U.S. Navy UAVs

Written by Ken Neubeck

In Action®

Squadron Signal® Publications

Cover Art by Don Greer

Line Illustrations by Matheu Spraggins

D1279093

(Front Cover) An RQ-2 Pioneer unmanned aerial vehicle leaves the USS *Missouri* to spot targets in Iraqi positions entrenched on Faylakâ Island, Kuwait, in February 1991.

(Back Cover) An X-47 Pegasus flies away after a bombing run. The Pegasus is currently under evaluation by the U.S. Navy for carrier deployment. Sea trials begin in 2011.

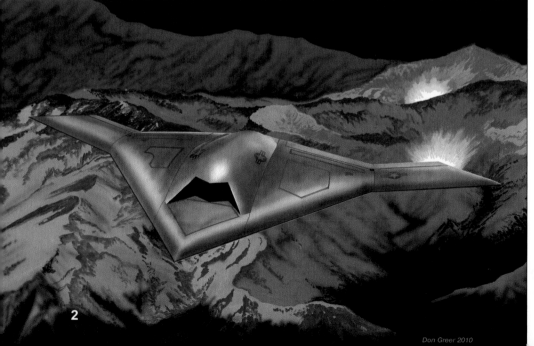

About the In Action® Series

In Action® books, despite the title of the genre, are books that trace the development of a single type of aircraft, armored vehicle, or ship from prototype to the final production variant. Experimental or "one-off" variants can also be included. Our first *In Action*® book was printed in 1971.

ISBN 978-0-89747-608-9

Copyright 2010 Squadron/Signal Publications
1115 Crowley Drive, Carrollton, TX 75006-1312 U.S.A.
Printed in the U.S.A.

Military/Combat Photographs and Snapshots

If you have any photos of aircraft, armor, soldiers, or ships of any nation, particularly wartime snapshots, please share them with us and help make Squadron/Signal's books all the more interesting and complete in the future. Any photograph sent to us will be copied and returned. Electronic images are preferred. The donor will be fully credited for any photos used. Please send them to:

Squadron/Signal Publications
1115 Crowley Drive
Carrollton, TX 75006-1312 U.S.A.
www.SquadronSignalPublications.com

(Title Page) A BQM-74 Chukar III target drone takes from a launcher using JATO rockets from the USS *O'Brien* in February of 2002. (U.S. Navy Photo by Ensign Lyn Niemer)

Acknowledgments

The author wishes to dedicate this book to his father, Ray, whose long career in aerospace began with work on the US Navy Lark missile program with Fairchild Industries. His encouragement has helped the author in his involvement in the aerospace field as well.

This project was an interesting challenge to try to capture as much information about the U.S. Navy's involvement in the field of unmanned aerial vehicles. The author is grateful to the following individuals for their contributions to this project; Gary Fisk, Robert Hammerquist, André Jans, Dennis R. Jenkins, Paul Negri, Ray Neubeck, and Josh Stoff. Also acknowledgement is given to the following organizations; Cradle of Aviation Museum, Air Force Armament Museum, National Naval Aviation Museum, New Jersey Naval Museum, Northrop Grumman, Patuxent River Naval Air Museum, U.S. Navy, U.S. Marine Corp and USAF.

Evolution of Unmanned Air Vehicles and U.S. Navy Involvement

Research on unmanned aerial vehicles (UAVs) began as far back as 1896 when Samuel P. Langley launched his UAV named Aerodrome Number 5 on a one-minute flight over the Potomac River. Since that time, UAV development has generally played second fiddle to manned aircraft platforms, although interest in UAVs began to grow during the latter part of the 20th Century. In the new millennium it has become apparent that UAVs will be taking over many tedious missions, such as coastal patrol, as well as many dangerous aerial reconnaissance missions that were formerly handled by human pilots.

The first unmanned military aircraft were flying bombs such as the Kettering "Bug" and the Sperry "Flying Bomb" that came out near the end World War I but achieved no operational success. As early as the 1930s, radio amateurs were operating radio-controlled (RC) hobby aircraft and model boats, using VHF-range frequencies. Techniques in recovery and landing that were developed with hobby aircraft later provided valuable information to military UAV programs, beginning in earnest in World War II.

During the Second World War, the U.S. Army QQ-2A and U.S. Navy TDD-1 target drone was developed for anti-aircraft practice. The secret Navy aircraft, the Interstate TDR-1, was an attack drone with a torpedo that was used on a limited basis in about a dozen attacks in the Pacific. Also during the war, radio-controlled B-17 and B-24 aircraft at the end of their service life were used in Project Aphrodite. The aircraft were equipped with TV cameras in the nose and loaded from cockpit to tail with up to 20,000 pounds of explosives. An on-board crew would get the planes airborne, switch control to a chase plane, and bail out. B-24 drones attacked the German submarine base at Heligoland in 1944, but in general, accidents and logistical difficulties made the extensive use of drones impractical.

The development of guided missiles, particularly those deployed on U.S. Navy submarines and surface ships, was another proving ground for remote-control aerial vehicles. Germany's introduction of the Vergeltungswaffe-1 (V-1 or "Buzz Bomb") in 1944, spurred the U.S. military to undertake major research and turn out a similar system through reverse-engineering. The resulting Loon missile developed by the United States Army Air Force was later deployed from U.S. Navy ships. After takeoff from ships, the Loon could be guided to its target by radio control aboard another airborne Navy plane.

In late 1944 the Japanese *kamikaze* suicide-bombers that were plaguing the fleet in the Pacific prompted the U.S. Navy to introduce the Lark anti-aircraft missile program. Under the program in early 1945, a system was developed in which a Lark surface-to-air missile would take off from a Navy ship and be guided to its target by control signals transmitted by FM or radar homing. A contract for the Lark was awarded to Fairchild Engine and Aircraft Corporation. Later, additional production work was also given to Convair. A Convair-built Lark took off from the USS *Norton Sound* in 1950 and successfully intercepted a moving target in the air. Later in 1950, however, the Lark program ended.

The Kettering "Bug," a flying bomb developed during World War I, met with little success. (USAF)

During World War II, this end-of-life B-17 aircraft was stripped down and loaded with bombs as part of Project Aphrodite. (National Archives via Dennis R. Jenkins)

This 1957 photo of a Lark missile with the author and his father, an engineer on the Lark program for the Fairchild Missile Division, was taken at a Long Island air show. (Ray Neubeck)

In 1954, testing began of the Fairchild AQM-41 Petrel, an air-launched jet-powered missile that used radar homing and carried a torpedo warhead. (André Jans)

During World War II, the United States Army Air Force contracted with Martin Aircraft for the development of the Matador turbojet-powered missile. The U.S. Navy followed suit with a similar system, the Chance Vought-manufactured Regulus cruise missile. The Regulus missile would be remote controlled from two guidance sources and could travel 500 miles to target. Regulus was to be in service for 10 years.

The U.S. Navy also developed the AQM-41 Petrel missile designed for attacks on surface vessels. The Peterel was intended as an air-launched jet missile powered by a Fairchild J44 turbojet engine and carried a torpedo warhead along with a radar homing guidance system located in the nose. The missile was capable of traveling at Mach 0.5 speeds and was typically carried by the Lockheed P-2 Neptune aircraft.

UAVs were well suited for use as reusable target drones and came to replace the obsolete aircraft that had previously played this role. The U.S. Air Force produced the first target drone, the Q-2A Ryan Firebee, in 1951 and the Navy and the Army followed suit. Another target drone that was developed later and is used up to the present day by the U.S. Navy was the Northrop BQM-74 Chukar. By the late 1950s, a number of US Army surveillance drone programs were cancelled before production but key concepts would later appear in Navy UAV designs such as the Fairchild SD-3.

It was during the Cold War that UAV development for reconnaissance really began. After two manned U-2 reconnaissance planes were shot down over the Soviet Union and Cuba in 1960, serious consideration was given to using UAVs for this mission.

The first reconnaissance UAV was the Ryan Model 147 Lightning Bug which was

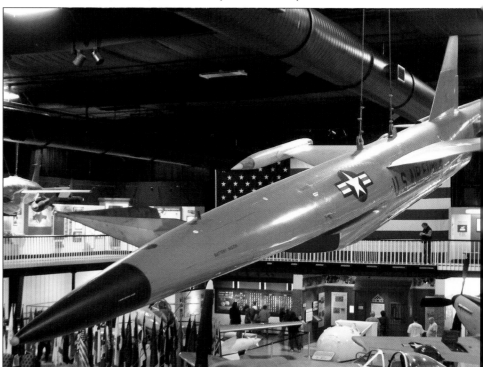

The original Ryan Firebee developed into several different drone platforms, including this USAF BQM-34F, Firebee II version. (Ken Neubeck)

developed from the Ryan Firebee. After completing testing in 1962, it entered into service in Vietnam for the US Air Force. The Lightning Bug flew over 3,400 missions during the war in Vietnam, taking on roles in reconnaissance, electronic warfare, and even dropping propaganda leaflets. Later models of the Lightning Bug flew several hundred more sorties in Vietnam, conducting airborne electronic intelligence, beginning in 1970.

Another project was the Gyrodyne QH-50 rotorcraft UAV. The QH-50 was a vertical takeoff and landing (VTOL) vehicle that could lift off from U.S. Navy destroyers in rough seas and deliver either two acoustic homing torpedoes or a nuclear depth charge for anti-submarine warfare. Over 700 different QH-50 models were made for the Navy.

During the Arab-Israeli October War of 1973, the Israelis used UAVs as tactical weapons, tricking Arab-operated SAM radars into thinking that they were full-sized aircraft and revealing themselves, allowing Israeli manned aircraft to attack the sites. In 1980, the Naval Research Laboratory started a test program for a long-duration expendable decoy (LODED) in which a one-half scale radio-controlled model was made but no further units were built.

For a time, the armed services were more interested in manned aircraft than in UAVs. In 1985, however, interest in UAVs would rebound with the RQ-2 Pioneer, a joint effort by Israeli Aircraft Industries and the AAI Corporation. The U.S. Navy successfully used the RQ-2, which saw significant action during Operation Desert Storm. By 1990, the flood gates were opened for many companies and teams to come up with practical UAV designs for different missions for the various US armed services.

The U.S. Navy has taken a major role in UAV development and is using the designation UAS or Unmanned Aerial System for the different systems currently under development. Roles for newer UAVs can differ between platforms with the main focus still being primarily in the area of reconnaissance and surveillance.

Indeed, the U.S. Navy sees two main advantages in using UAS over manned aircraft – coverage time and cost effectiveness. A traditional manned aircraft can remain aloft up to about eight hours, refueling as required, but then the issue of pilot fatigue arises. With UAS, however, an unmanned vehicle can stay airborne for two or three days, as ground operators rotate on regular shifts, an arrangement impossible for manned aircraft.

Unmanned aerial vehicles use less fuel and cost less to fly than manned vehicles. Also, the costs of aircraft loss and crew training, are significantly lower with UAVs, making UAVs cost-effective compliments to manned aircraft for the U.S. Navy.

In general, the size of a UAV dictates the type of mission it will undertake. Smaller UAV designs such as the Pioneer and the ScanEagle are used for short-range, over-the-hill type reconnaissance missions. Larger UAVs would typically have longer wing spans for longer loiter time and would be designed to hold more fuel for longer-range surveillance and patrol missions. Among the larger UAVs is the Global Hawk Broad Area Maritime Surveillance (BAMS) aircraft used for long-duration coastal patrols.

In the future, newer roles such as limited interdiction missions and bombing are also being considered for UAVs. Some vehicles will be capable of carrying a weapon pod or bomb rack. This role will prove valuable in high-risk battleground areas where loss of a manned aircraft would be a severe blow.

A joint effort of AAI and Israel Aircraft Industry, the RQ-2 Pioneer was deployed by the U.S. Navy during the 1980s. (Ken Neubeck)

The MQ-8 Fire Scout UAV is currently deployed from U.S. Navy frigates and will eventually operate from littoral combat ships (LCS). (U.S. Navy photo by Kurt Lengfield)

Curtiss-Sperry Flying Bomb

Within a few years of the introduction of the airplane, inventor Elmer Sperry and his son Lawrence looked into the idea of creating radio-controlled aircraft without using pilots. Initially, they teamed up with Peter Hewitt to develop for the U.S. Navy an aerial torpedo that would be known as the Hewitt-Sperry automatic airplane. The idea was to use the aerial torpedo to attack submarine bases in Germany.

Radio technology was not well developed at the time, however, and other practical issues arose would arise with the Curtiss N-9 seaplanes used in the project. Sperry undertook the work at its Copiague, Long Island, facility, and an autopilot-equipped aircraft did fly successfully in September of 1917 with a human pilot onboard to fly the takeoff. The Navy, however, never allocated funds for production of the aircraft.

In October of 1917, Sperry placed and order with the Curtiss Aeroplane and Motor Company to make six unique, 500-pound aircraft with a top speed of 90 mph that could carry 1,000 pounds of explosive. This aircraft would be known as the Curtiss-Sperry flying bomb. From November 1917 through January 1918, five flight tests ended in crashes and, after additional mishaps, it was determined that some additional flight test data were needed. A crude open-air wind-tunnel test model was created when an aircraft was mounted atop a Marmon automobile and driven along a parkway on Long Island. This testing resulted in adjustments of the flight controls, and the lengthening of the fuselage by two feet. Despite these improvements, eventually all six Curtiss-Sperry flying bomb aircraft would be depleted as a result of crashes and with the end of World War I, the Navy took over the program from Sperry, but undertook no further work.

In 1918, railroad tracks were unsuccessfully tested as a possible takeoff platform for the aircraft. (Sperry archives via Cradle of Aviation)

Sperry attached a modified Curtiss aircraft to the top of this Marmon automobile to gather wind-tunnel data by riding along the parkways of Long Island. A car successfully served as a takeoff platform on one occasion. (Sperry archives via Cradle of Aviation)

This Sperry-designed auto-pilot control system was installed into the cockpit of the flying bomb aircraft. It consisted of gyroscopes, servo motors, and stabilizers. (Sperry archives via Cradle of Aviation)

JB-2 Loon Guided Missile

The German V-1 Buzz Bomb rocket that appeared as a terror weapon over England in June of 1944 would cause a revolution in the area of unmanned aerial bombs. The V-1 was a very crude rocket system that would lose power and drop on its target once a preset distance had been traversed. An unexploded V-1 was sent from Europe to American engineers at Wright Field in Ohio to reverse-engineer the pulse-jet engine design. This undertaking resulted in a contract being awarded to Republic to make two prototype units with the first flight taking place at Eglin AFB, Florida, in October of 1944. The Loon thus became the first U.S. unmanned guided missile initially carrying Army's the designation JB-2.

Production of the Loon airframe was awarded to Republic Aviation Corporation, while Ford produced the pulsejet engine that allowed the Loon to travel as fast as 420 mph at a range of 150 miles. The pulsejet engine was mounted in a pod located above the fuselage of the missile, in much the same manner as on the V-1 rocket. The rocket had wings and a tail section along with a lower assembly that held four rockets for use in Jet Fuel Assisted Takeoff (JATO).

The U.S. Navy was significantly interested in the program from the start, even though the Army actually undertook much of the development. The Navy viewed the Loon as a weapon that it could potentially launch from its ships and submarines.

Republic built a total of 1,385 JB-2 Loons for the U.S. Army and Navy. Plans for the U.S. invasion of Japan called for aircraft carriers to launch Loons in support of the landings, but Japan's surrender in the end forestalled that use of the JB-2.

Although production of the Loon for the Army stopped shortly after the end of World War II, the Navy continued its testing of existing Loon missiles at Wendover Field in Utah. The U.S. Navy version of the Loon was initially designated the KUW-1 and in February of 1947 it became the first cruise missile to be launched from a submarine when a KUW-1 took off from the submarine *Cusk* off Pt. Magu, California.

Further testing continued, with the Navy re-designating the missile LTV-2. Then, in 1948, the final Navy version of the Loon was designated the LTV-N-2, the name that stuck until the program ended in 1950. The experience gathered from work with the Loon would then go on to contribute to the next Navy missile program, the Regulus cruise missile.

Specifications

Length:	25 feet, 4 inches
Wingspan:	17 feet, 4 inches
Gross weight:	4,800 pounds
Powerplant:	1 × Ford Pulsejet
Max takeoff weight:	360 pounds
Maximum speed:	420 mph
Range:	150 miles

A prototype Loon missile undergoes tests using railroad tracks for launching at Wendover Field, Utah, in 1945. The U.S. reverse-engineered the V-1 Buzz Bomb to produce the JB-2 Loon. (Republic archives via Cradle of Aviation)

As on the German V-1, the thrust needed to carry the Loon missile to its target comes from a pulsejet engine that is mounted on the top of the fuselage towards the rear of the aircraft. (Ken Neubeck)

Final assembly of the JB-2 Loon began in 1945 at the Republic company facility in Farmingdale, Long Island. (Republic archives via Cradle of Aviation)

The U.S. Navy initially tested the Loon aboard surface ships, as seen here. Later it was launched from submarines. (Republic archives via Cradle of Aviation)

U.S. Navy personnel check the four JATO rocket boosters attached to a structure located under the lower fuselage of the Loon. The JATO boosters help the Loon take off from the ship. (Republic archives via Cradle of Aviation)

The first KUW-1 Loon submarine launch was from the submarine *Cusk* in 1947. This Loon is taking off from unidentified sub using JATO boosters, as indicated by the aircraft's quadruple exhaust stream. (Republic archives via Cradle of Aviation)

The initial paint scheme for the early-production Loon missiles was white with the engine section painted black, as in this display model at Point Magu, California. (André Jans)

Later-production models of the Loon also featured vertical black and white markings on the tail and rudder flight-control surfaces. (Ken Neubeck)

This exhibit at the Cradle of Aviation museum shows the paint scheme on later-production Loons: yellow with U.S. insignia and a serial number on the nose. (Ken Neubeck)

A serial number is painted on both sides of the nose. The JATO boosters were attached to the bracket located on the bottom of the fuselage between the wings. (Ken Neubeck)

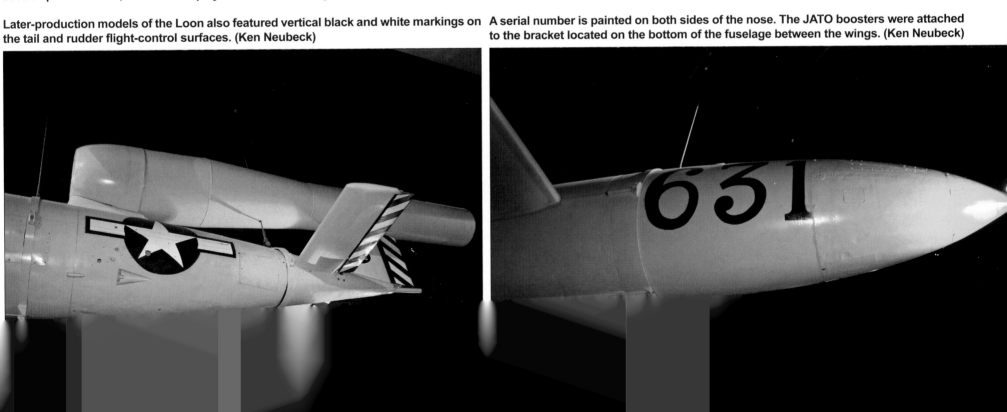

Regulus Cruise Missile

Key design features of the guided cruise missiles developed at the end of World War II were later incorporated in the designs of UAVs. The U.S. Navy Regulus cruise missile was the first UAV of its kind used by the Navy.

In 1943, the U.S. Army Air Force awarded a contract to Martin Aircraft to develop a turbojet-powered subsonic guided missile to be called Matador. Not to be outdone, the Navy wanted to have its own guided missile program and worked quickly to come up with the Regulus missile that Chance Vought would manufacture. After some debate regarding the feasibility of having two different missile programs, each powered by the same turbojet engine, development of the Regulus moved ahead. The Regulus initially required only two guidance systems and it could be recovered after test firings.

The Regulus was 32 feet long, had an extended wingspan of 21 feet, and a single vertical tail section. To aid in the assembly process and minimize weight, the Regulus featured a modular air frame made of a composite material called Metalite, which was essentially, a thin skin of aluminum covering a balsa wood core. The Regulus was powered by an Allison J33-A-14 turbojet engine along with two Jet Fuel Assisted Takeoff (JATO) booster rockets that allowed it to travel at supersonic speed with a range of 500 miles. It carried a 3,000-pound warhead, usually the W5 or W27. Regulus missiles were painted in navy blue with white lettering with the U.S. star insignia painted on the nose. A missile launcher facilitated takeoff of the Regulus from submarines and surface ships.

The first submarine missile launch occurred in July of 1953 when the USS *Tunny* used a missile launcher on its deck to send a Regulus aloft. The Regulus could be carried by five U.S. Navy submarines, two of which, the USS *Growler* and USS *Grayback,* were specifically built for the Regulus. These two submarines could each carry four Regulus missiles. Later, the nuclear-powered USS *Halibut* was capable of carrying five of the missiles. The goal was to always have four Regulus available and ready to fire at any one time during the nuclear deterrent patrols conducted by these submarines. The Regulus was on board for a total of 40 strategic deterrent patrols mounted between 1959 and 1964.

A Regulus trainer was developed that consisted essentially of a UAV-based system in which a control box was used to control the missile's direction. The trainer Regulus incorporated a landing gear system and drogue parachute to allow the craft to land. Thus, even though this was a missile system, many of the principles used in UAV programs later

on would be developed with the trainer.

In addition to being deployed from submarines, the Regulus was deployed from U.S. Navy cruisers with the first launch taking place from the USS *Los Angeles* in 1955. Four cruisers carried the missile while on patrol in the Pacific Ocean and eventually, 10 aircraft carriers would be configured to carry the missile as well, with the first carrier launch from the USS *Saratoga*. When launched from aircraft carriers, the missile could be guided to its target by carrier-based pilots using remote-control equipment.

A second generation, known as the Regulus II was developed and successfully tested. It had a range of 1,200 miles and a speed of Mach 2, but the program was cancelled in favor of the Polaris ballistic nuclear missile that could also be launched from submarines.

A total of 514 Regulus missiles were built and saw service during the period from 1955 through 1964.

Specifications

Length:	32 feet
Wingspan:	21 feet
Empty weight:	10,685 pounds
Gross weight:	13,685 pounds
Powerplant:	1 Allison J33-A-14 turbojet, 2 booster rockets
Maximum speed:	Mach 1
Range:	500 miles

This Regulus missile mounted on a maintenance carrier is displayed near the USS *Ling* submarine at the New Jersey Naval Museum in Hackensack. (Ken Neubeck)

This Chance Vought ad shows the Regulus trainer version that was remote-controlled. (Chance Vought archives)

Navy personnel prepare a Regulus for test firing at a ground base in 1953. The Regulus was first deployed into U.S. Navy service in 1953. (U.S. Navy)

The Regulus is mounted here on the USS *Grayback* (SSG-574), with crewmen positioned at the bow. (US Navy)

The Regulus is poised to launch at approximately 30° in elevation. This model on the USS *Growler* submarine is static and does not have the two rear JATO rocket boosters attached. (Ken Neubeck)

On submarines, the Regulus takes off from a dual-rail launcher mounted on the deck. The USS *Growler* submarine exhibit is located next to the Intrepid Air & Space Museum in New York City. (Ken Neubeck)

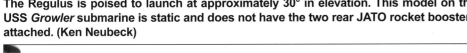

A 3,000-pound warhead was contained in the forward compartment behind the nose of the Regulus. The end of the dual rail launcher assembly is visible here. (Ken Neubeck)

The wingspan of the Regulus measures 22 feet when the wings are fully extended and 14 feet when they are stowed. (Ken Neubeck)

The tail section of the Regulus is made up of a single vertical section constructed of a Metalite shell over sheet metal ribs. (Ken Neubeck)

The missile launcher consists of a set of rails mounted on a base assembly that could pivot in circular fashion on the deck of the submarine. (Ken Neubeck)

During ground transport, the Regulus is positioned on a cart that is used to carry the missile to the submarine. JATO boosters area attached to this model. (Ken Neubeck)

This view of one of the JATO rocket booster on the right side of the Regulus shows a body section and an exhaust section. (Ken Neubeck)

The JATO is attached to the body of the Regulus by a bracket located in the front section and positioning clamps located in the rear. (Ken Neubeck)

A center stud and two clamps connect the rear of the JATO to the Regulus. (Ken Neubeck)

The nose inlet of the Regulus is seen here from the front. (Ken Neubeck)

Ryan BQM-34 Firebee Target Drone

In 1948, the U.S. Air Force put out a request to Ryan Aeronautical Company to develop a jet-powered gunnery target drone. Ryan developed a prototype designated as the XQ-2 that flew in early 1951. The drone featured a swept-wing and tail design along with an inlet located on the lower nose. This drone could be either air-launched or ground-launched with a single Jet-Fuel-Assisted Takeoff (JATO) booster.

The first version used by the U.S. Navy was the KDA-1, which was similar to the Q-2A version employed by the Air Force, except that it was powered by a Fairchild J44-R-20B turbojet. Improved variants of the KDA-1, the XKDA-2 and XKDA-3, followed the initial version, and these paved the way for the emergence of the KDA-4, with an upgraded J44 engine.

In the late 1950s, the Air Force awarded Ryan a contract to improve the Firebee and after some designation changes it wound up redesignated as the BQM-34A. The two models of Navy Firebee that were in service were initially redesignated as the AQM-34B and the AQM-34C. Eventually the Navy would adopt the BQM-34A designation for the model incorporating the improved Continental J69-T-20A turbojet, which had more thrust than the previous model.

In 1965, the U.S. Navy awarded a contract to Ryan for the supersonic third-generation Firebee II, which first took to the air in 1968. This version, dubbed the BQM-34E, looked significantly different from the original Firebee, but incorporated the same engine and control system.

The Firebee is outfitted with various control systems that can give it the maneuverability of a fighter aircraft. The Firebee can also be equipped with countermeasure systems as well as radar enhancement devices that allow it to emulate a wide range of combat aircraft. The Firebee can mount wingtip thermal flares that cause heat-seeking missiles to aim for the wingtip rather than the engine exhaust, allowing the target drone to be saved and used another day.

During the 1970s, the Navy upgraded its BQM-34As with improved avionics, and the resulting aircraft were then designated BQM-34S. Later on during the early 1980s, the Navy would also refit these drones with the improved J69-T-41A engine, providing 1,920 pounds (871kg) of thrust.

The U.S. Navy is able to launch the Firebee from ground-based stations or from the Lockheed DC-130 Hercules drone controller aircraft, which can carry four drones on underwing pylons. The drone uses a parachute that reduces damage to the Firebee from ground impact. After a target exercise is completed, a helicopter can recover the drone while it is still in the air. If it is ditched in water, the Firebee is also able to float for an extended period of time, and it can also emit a green marker dye to facilitate easier spotting by helicopter crews during recovery.

Production of the original BQM-34A ended in 1982 but the line was reopened in 1986 to produce BQM-34S drones for both the U.S. Air Force and the U.S. Navy. Recent retrofits of this model include the improved J85-GE-100 engine along with improved avionics. In recent years, some Firebees have even been outfitted with a Global Positioning System (GPS) to improve flight control and tracking during target practice.

In 1999, Northrop Grumman purchased Ryan Aeronautical, and moved Northrop's BQM-34 program to Ryan's San Diego location to join with programs such as the Firebee, creating a new division to handle Northrop Grumman's unmanned systems. Thousands of Firebees have been manufactured for the U.S. armed services over the period of 55 years during which the aircraft has been in service. The U.S. military still continues to use Firebee as a target drone in the present day.

Specifications (BQM-44A Model)

Length:	22 feet
Wingspan:	12 feet, 10 inches
Empty weight:	1,500 pounds
Gross weight:	2,500 pounds
Powerplant:	1 × Continental J69-T-41A
Maximum speed:	710 mph
Endurance:	1 hour 15 min
Service ceiling:	60,000 feet

This USAF Firebee in the Eglin AFB Museum, Florida, represents the basic model and shape of the aircraft. The U.S. Air Force and the U.S. Navy have been using the Firebee target drone for over 50 years. (Ken Neubeck)

The JATO booster propels the drone upwards to the desired altitude, at which point the drone's engine is switched on. (Northrop Grumman)

Firebees can be launched from the U.S. Navy DC-130, which can carry two drones under each wing. Launch from aircraft precludes the need for JATO, since the Firebee engine is started upon its release from the airplane's wing pylon. (Northop Grumman)

The Ryan BQM-34 Firebee has been in U.S. service for 55 years and is used by USAF and the U.S. Navy as the primary target drone for gunnery practice. The design continues to be improved with engine upgrades as well the introduction of GPS to aid in control. The Firebee shown above is using JATO booster mounted on the lower fuselage to take off from a ground launcher. (Northrop Grumman)

Two orange BQM-34S Firebees are mounted under the wing of a DC-130 for air-to-air target practice. (U.S. Navy photo by PHCS R.L. Lawson)

The Firebee paint scheme can be either orange or gray. This particular Firebee features a shark's mouth, and displays several mission-completion markings as well. (Ken Neubeck)

A Navy SH-3G Sea King helicopter from VC-5 is in the process of retrieving a BQM-34S Firebee that has just emitted green marker dye for easier spotting. (U.S. Navy photo by PHC Lawrence B. Foster)

The tail section of this early-model BQM-34A actually has an adjustment for pitch that is located on the outside of the vertical section. (Ken Neubeck)

16

MQM-36 Shelduck

The Radioplane Company developed its OQ-2 target drone during World War II and followed up after the war with a series of target drones that were powered by a single piston engine. These drones were designated as the basic training target (BTT) drone.

The U.S. Navy version of this drone was the Quail with an initial KD2R designation. In 1952, Radioplane was bought out by Northrop and in 1963, the KD2R-1 was renamed the MQM-36 Shelduck by the U.S. Navy.

Powered by a 95-horsepower McCulloch piston engine, the MQM-36 was the fastest and most sophisticated of the BTT family. Launch was accomplished by JATO booster or bungee catapult, with recovery by parachute that was installed in the aircraft. Altogether, a total of 73,000 BTT-type drones were built under different designations for different services and different nations.

Specifications

Length:	12 feet, 8 inches
Height:	2 feet, 6 inches
Wingspan:	11 feet, 6 inches
Empty weight:	271 pounds
Max takeoff weight:	360 pounds
Powerplant:	McCulloch O-100-2, 90 HP
Maximum speed:	230 mph
Endurance:	1 hour
Range:	210 miles
Service ceiling:	23,000 feet

The KD2R Navy drone appears in front of Army drones at the Western Aircraft Museum. (Gary Fisk)

MQM-39 Target Drone

The Beech-manufactured MQM-39 was a target drone whose appearance resembled that of the MQM-36. The MQM-39 was originally designated as the KDB-1 by the U.S. Navy after production started in 1959.

The drone could be launched either by a catapult or rocket-assisted launcher. It was controlled in flight by a radio command guidance system, and it could be recovered through the use a single drogue parachute. The KDB-1 was used by the Navy for air-to-air and ground-to-air anti-aircraft missile and gunnery training.

In June of 1963, the Navy redesignated the KDB-1 as MQM-39A. Production ended in the early 1970s after almost 1,000 of these drones had been built for the U.S. Navy.

Beech also made other target drones, such as the AQM-37, for the U.S. Navy, beginning in 1963. More than 4,200 AQM-37s were built.

Specifications

Length:	15 feet, 1 inch
Height:	3 feet, 4 inches
Wingspan:	13 feet
Empty weight:	560 pounds
Max takeoff weight:	664 pounds
Powerplant:	McCulloch TC6150-J-2, 125 HP
Maximum speed:	350 mph
Endurance:	1 hour
Range:	300 miles
Service ceiling:	43,000 feet

Aboard ship for gunnery practice, this Beech KDB target drone resembles the KD2R target drone. (U.S. Navy)

Gyrodyne QH-50 DASH Rotor UAV

One of the Navy's more innovative UAVs was the Gyrodyne QH-50 unmanned rotor aircraft. The QH-50 was designated the DASH and it was the first UAV designed to carry a payload as part of the Navy's anti-submarine warfare mission.

This UAV was developed in response to the U.S. Navy's need for a vehicle that could take off from a warship and detect the presence of nearby Soviet submarines. Manned helicopters were considered impractical because of the difficulty of taking off from small destroyer decks during high sea conditions. The first unmanned system to take on such missions was the QH-50A, which came to be designated the Drone Anti-Submarine Helicopter or DASH.

The DASH was made by the Gyrodyne company, which was founded in the North Shore, Long Island community of St. James in 1951. The owner, Peter Papadakos, had helped perfect a unique, simple, powerful, and light coaxial rotor for helicopters. Papadakos applied the design not only to his Model 2B helicopter but also in the one-man Rotorcycle. This design became the basis for a contract awarded by the U.S. Navy in 1958 to develop an unmanned drone that could take off from a destroyer under rough sea conditions and could deliver anti-submarine weapons.

The DASH model evolved further, incorporating a heavy fuel turbine engine made by Boeing. It was also fitted to carry two MK44 acoustic homing torpedoes, or a MK17 nuclear depth charge. The first real production DASH model was the QH-50C and was initially deployed on the destroyer USS *Buck* in January 1963. Vibration problems delayed overall deployment of 80 drones until a fix, developed in July 1963, allowed resumption of the program. A total of 377 C models were delivered to the Navy.

The next DASH model, the QH-50D, dispensed with the tail, which was no longer needed for stability. It used a more reliable Boeing T50-BO-12 turbine engine, and had upgraded avionics. In all, 373 QH-50Ds were supplied to the U.S. Navy. Another 16 QH-50D models were supplied to the Japanese Maritime Self-Defense Force.

Using the controller to fly the DASH was hard, due to the series of complicated maneuvers that it required. Moreover, since much of the system was non-redundant, a single command failure could cause the loss of the drone. The GAO reported that 80 percent of QH-50s were lost due to ship-based or airborne electronic-system failures.

As the war in Vietnam unfolded, it became clear that anti-submarine activity was not required and that the Navy would have to find another mission for the DASH. In January 1965, the QH-50 was fitted with video and film cameras for reconnaissance and surveillance work in Vietnam. Under Project Snoopy, DASH spotted targets for guns on Navy destroyers. The drone would fly in environments much too hostile for manned aircraft. Project Snoopy ended in 1970 and the DASH was removed from U.S. destroyers. At that time, the Navy estimated that it had lost 411 of the total 746 QH-50 C and D models that had been built. Prototypes for a model E had been developed, but the project ended in 1969 when the Navy ordered removal of all QH-50 models from service.

Since leaving Vietnam, the surviving QH-50s have served until today as target drones at the Naval Air Station in China Lake and the U.S. Army's White Sands Missile Range.

A QH-50C DASH with two homing torpedoes lifts off from the deck of the USS *Hazelwood*. A major advantage of the DASH over manned rotary aircraft was its ability to take off and land in rough seas. (Gyrodyne archives via Cradle of Aviation)

Specifications (QH-50D Model)

Height:	9 feet, 8 inches
Empty weight:	1,035 pounds
Loaded weight:	2,330 pounds
Max takeoff weight:	2,303 pounds
Powerplant:	1× Boeing T50-8A turboshaft
Maximum speed:	92 mph
Range:	82 miles
Service ceiling:	16,000 feet

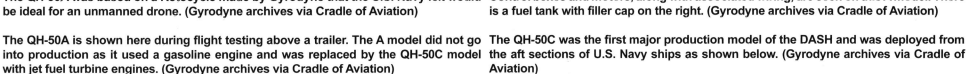

The QH-50A was based on a Rotocycle made by Gyrodyne that the U.S. Navy felt would be ideal for an unmanned drone. (Gyrodyne archives via Cradle of Aviation)

The QH-50A is shown here during flight testing above a trailer. The A model did not go into production as it used a gasoline engine and was replaced by the QH-50C model with jet fuel turbine engines. (Gyrodyne archives via Cradle of Aviation)

Control boxes and motors, along with associated wiring, are seen on this A model. There is a fuel tank with filler cap on the right. (Gyrodyne archives via Cradle of Aviation)

The QH-50C was the first major production model of the DASH and was deployed from the aft sections of U.S. Navy ships as shown below. (Gyrodyne archives via Cradle of Aviation)

The C model of the QH-50 had a tail section that consisted of two vertical stabilizers attached to the airframe of the UAV. (Ken Neubeck)

This front view of the QH-50C shows the front of the torpedoes as well as the main housing of the engine along with both exhaust ports. (Ken Neubeck)

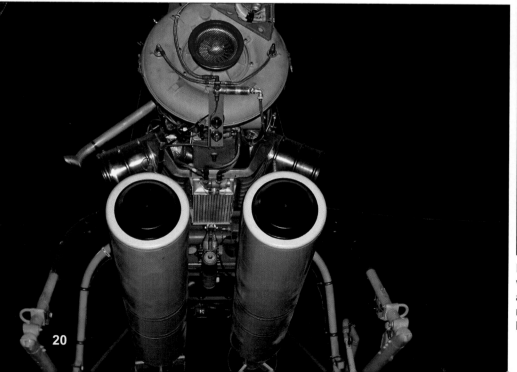

Located between the two homing torpedoes is the lower fluid pan for the engine, along with blue and red coded flexible hydraulic lines. Behind the pan is a charge cylinder along with some wire cable that feeds through the structure. These items make up the release mechanism for dropping each of the homing torpedoes that are attached to the DASH by means of a pair of metallic straps. (Ken Neubeck)

One engine exhaust is located on the left side of the QH-50C. The left side of the fuel tank is painted orange and there is a red landing light on the forward rails. (Ken Neubeck)

The landing rail and the right side fuel tank are painted light green. Located on the forward rails is a green landing light. (Ken Neubeck)

Looking at the QH-50C from the rear shows the unique two-color paint scheme that was used for the DASH where the landing rails on the left are painted orange or bright red and the landing rails on the right are painted light green. The rails straddle a set of two MK44 acoustic homing torpedoes that are connected to the bottom of the airframe and used to track submarines. Each torpedo has its own propeller located at the end and is released from the DASH by remote signal. (Ken Neubeck)

The landing struts connect to framework that surrounds the engine. The USS *Stickell* markings refer to the destroyer on which this DASH was based. (Ken Neubeck)

A side view of the front of the QH-50C model shows the electric cooling motor with associated ducts, along with the left side engine exhaust. (Ken Neubeck)

The QH-50 is operated by using a stand-alone control box that is mounted on a pedestal bolted to the deck of the ship. The Gyrodyne-made control box transmitted radio-control signals to the DASH after launch. (Ken Neubeck)

The joy stick on the right side of the control box is used to operate the DASH. There is a compass located in the middle of the box and an altitude indicator to the left. (Ken Neubeck)

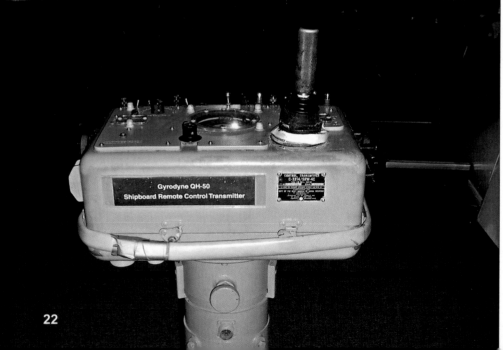

Unlike the earlier C model, the QH-50D had no tail section. (Ken Neubeck)

A lower set of rotors has been removed from this QH-50D aircraft. (Ken Neubeck)

Under the blades on both sides of the shaft are scissor assemblies. Linkages maintain proper blade alignment between the top and bottom blade sets. (Ken Neubeck)

The rear of the QH-50D model has three rows of connectors to which various cables from electrical subsystems are wired. (Ken Neubeck)

With the payload removed from under this QH-50D, the set of bomb rack-type attachments that normally holds the payload is visible. (Ken Neubeck)

A QH-50C model is shown here in flight. Gyrodyne built a total of 377 C-models for the U.S. Navy. (Gyrodyne archives via Cradle of Aviation)

This C-model DASH UAV hangs from the ceiling in the Cradle of Aviation Museum on Long Island. (Ken Neubeck)

The tail section was eliminated from the D model version of the DASH. In all, 373 D-models were supplied to the U.S. Navy, and 16 more were delivered to the Japanese Maritime Self-Defense Force. (Gyrodyne archives via Cradle of Aviation)

The DASH ended Navy service in 1970, but the QH-50D has continued to be used as a target drone at White Sands AFB in New Mexico until the present day. (Gyrodyne archives via Cradle of Aviation)

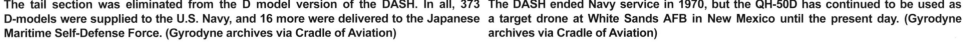

BQM-74 Chukar Target Drone

The BQM-74 Chukar is a series of aerial target drones produced by Northrop Grumman (formerly Northrop) for the U.S. Navy. After three major revisions, the Chukar remains active in U.S. Navy service.

In the early 1960s, the U.S. Navy was in need of a new target drone and Northrop developed a prototype designated NV-105. The original design, which featured a delta wing, first flew in 1964. In 1965, the delta wing was replaced by a straight wing design for enhanced stability and in 1968 the drone went into production as the MQM-74A or the Chukar I. The MQM-74 had a cigar-shaped fuselage with straight mid-mounted wings and a conventional tail configuration. Powered by a Williams International WR24-6 turbojet engine, it was equipped with a parachute for water recovery and was painted bright orange to make it easier to locate. The drone could take off either from the ground or from a ship using a JATO booster. The U.S. Navy purchased over 1,800 of this model drone, and NATO, the Royal Navy, and the Italian Navy bought several hundred more. Production lasted into the early 1970s.

Eventually, the Navy came to feel a need for a faster version that could provide more training challenges for the jets being developed at the time. Northrop responded with the Chukar II, which used an uprated Williams WR24-7 turbojet engine and could reach a top speed of 590 mph. All told, 1,400 Chukar IIs were built for the U.S. Navy, and for Great Britain, West Germany, Spain, and other NATO countries.

By 1978, the U.S. Navy wanted an even more advanced drone and Northrop developed the BQM-74C Chukar III. This UAV incorporates microprocessor-type technology that allows the UAV to be programmed for more advanced flight operations. This version differed from the previous model in that it could also be either ground launched or air launched by the DC-130 or other aircraft. Initially the Williams WR24-7A powered the new drone, but in 1986, the J400-WR-404 engine was substituted, and eventually the Chukar III's designation was changed to BQM-74E. More than 1,600 of this model have been built.

The Chukar III was used to create diversions during Operation Desert Storm, the war against Iraq in 1991. A team was quickly assembled to form the 4468th Tactical Reconnaissance Group to support the use of the Chukar III in the war, in which the code name for the use of BQM-74s as decoys was Project Scathe Mean. Instead of being launched by air, ground launchers sent the drones into the sky. Each Chukar III was equipped with radar enhancement devices to give the UAV a signature similar to that of an an attack aircraft. During the second wave of air attacks on Baghdâd on 17 January 1991, 37 Chukar IIIs were successfully launched as diversionary vehicles. When Iraqi air defense radar probed the drones, allied aircraft were able to spot and strike the Iraqi radar sites. The use of these drones was key for the successful prosecution of the war, since they were instrumental in minimizing allied aircraft loses during the early missions over Iraq.

After Northrop merged with with Grumman to form Northrop Grumman Corporation in 1994, a swept-wing BQM-74F variant with an upgraded engine was developed that had a top speed of Mach 0.93.

U.S. Navy ships continue to use portable launchers mounted on rear decks to send the Chukar aloft for target practice. (Northrop Grumman)

Specifications (BQM-74C Model)

Length:	13 feet
Height:	2.3 feet
Wingspan:	5.8 feet
Gross weight:	455 pounds
Powerplant:	1 × Williams J400-WR-404
Speed:	515 knots
Endurance:	78 miles
Service ceiling:	40,000 feet

Chukar III UAVs are being assembled in the final assembly area of the Northrop Grumman facility. (Northrop Grumman)

Chukar III UAVs undergo a series of test firings in the desert. The Chukar III launcher is similar to that used for the Regulus in the 1950s. (Northrop Grumman)

The full impact of the JATO booster to aid in takeoff is vividly apparent. After the booster, the Chukar flies on the turbojet engine. (Northrop Grumman)

The target drone flies just above the water as U.S. Navy guns fire at it. Near misses allow for drone recovery. (Northrop Grumman)

The crew positions a Chukar on a launch trajectory on a rocket launcher located at the rear of their ship. All of the Chukar drones in this photo have white JATO rockets on each side of the fuselage to aid in the launch. (Northrop Grumman)

JATO boosters on each side of the Chukar hurl the drone skyward off the ship. (Northrop Grumman)

JATO assist rockets launch the Chukar at a 30-degree angle off the ship. (Northrop Grumman)

The Chukar is a recoverable drone. When it runs out of fuel or if the engine shuts off, a parachute deploys from the center of the top of the fuselage. The parachute allows the Chukar to descend into the water where it will float; awaiting recovery by the ship after the exercise is completed. (Northrop Grumman)

Sea hooks are used in the recovery of the Chukar from water. Crewmen use sea hooks to catch the parachute lines and then use a winch to reel the drone up onto the boat. The drone appears basically intact and will be ready to fly again on a future mission. (U.S. Navy)

A Chukar III BQM-74E sits on a maintenance carrying cart ready for loading onto the bomb rack of a DC-130 aircraft, which will later release the drone in flight. (André Jans)

Two attachment brackets hold the Chukar to the bomb rack. The lower inlet cooling scoop on the fuselage is visible above the drone. (Northrop Grumman)

This DC-130 has two Chukars on its left wing, one on each pylon. There are two more on the right wing. A total of four can be carried per mission. (Northrop Grumman)

This Chukar is ready to be launched. Right after the DC-130 releases it, the Chukar's engines will fire up, shooting the UAV ahead of the airplane. (Northrop Grumman)

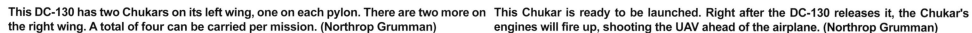

In addition to the DC-130, other military aircraft, including USAF fighters as well as the Navy A-6 shown above, can launch the Chukar. (Northrop Grumman)

The newest version of the Chukar, the BQM-74F, features swept wings and an upgraded engine that allows the drone to reach Mach 0.93 speed. (Northrop Grumman)

After it is released from the bomb rack of the DC-130, the Chukar drops straight down from the aircraft and its engine is activated. The Chukar then speeds ahead of the DC-130 to come into range as a target for Navy fighters in training. Besides serving as a target drone, the Chukar was used as a decoy during Operation Desert Storm in 1991, drawing attention from Iraqi air defense radars that would then be exposed for attack from Allied strike aircraft. (Northrop Grumman)

RQ-2 Pioneer UAV

The RQ-2 Pioneer represents a major turning point in UAV development as it became a practical means for providing real-time surveillance imaging in an aircraft that was easier to maintain and transport. The Pioneer signalled the Navy's new attitude to UAVs, which were no longer regarded as mere target drones.

The U.S. Navy observed Israel's successful use of UAVs during the early 1980s and promoted a fast-pace procurement of interim UAV capability in 1985. The goal was to develop a UAV that initially would be launched from Navy *Iowa*-class battleships and be able to provide imagery intelligence of targets for the spotters for Navy gunfire support. A joint effort of AAI Corporation and Israel Aircraft Industries produced the RQ-2 Pioneer UAV that could do short-range reconnaissance and surveillance both for ship-based operations for the Navy and land-based operations for the Marines.

The portable Pioneer RQ-2 has a 16-foot wingspan and 14-foot length and can be launched either from ships using a rocket-assisted catapult or from small runways on land. It can be recovered either by a net on a ship or via an arresting hook and landing cable system on a runway. Each Pioneer UAV is fitted with a gimbaled EO/IR sensor that relays analog video in real time via C-band line-of-sight data link.

The Pioneer skipped the typical development phase and the Navy and Marines procured nine systems, each with eight UAVs, beginning in 1986. The USS *Iowa* first deployed the Pioneer in December 1986 and it later saw service on other warships and LPD-class vessels. The Pioneer experienced a number of problems that resulted in crashes, however. One of the biggest headaches was the fact that electromagnetic signals from ship systems interfered with the Pioneer control system. The Navy pumped an additional $50 million into the program and brought the Pioneer up to a minimum operating standard.

Six separate Pioneer system groups were deployed to the Persian Gulf during Operation Desert Shield in 1990. Pioneers flew 545 surveillance missions, logging almost 1,700 flying hours, averaging three hours a mission. During Desert Storm operations in 1991, the Pioneer flew 313 combat reconnaissance missions, accumulating almost 1,100 flight hours, again with an average time of three hours per mission. Twelve Pioneers were lost during Desert Storm, and another 18 were damaged during combat action.

On one occasion, a Pioneer spotted the fire of 16-inch guns of the USS *Missouri* onto Iraqi positions on Faylakâ Island, Kuwait. After U.S. Naval artillery devastated the Iraqi defenses, the Pioneer was intentionally flown at low altitude to alert the Iraqis that they were being targeted again. The sight of the Pioneer UAVs prompted the Iraqi survivors to surrender, in what became a well-publicized wartime demonstration of the effectiveness of UAVs in spotting targets for Navy ships.

Since Desert Storm, the Pioneer RQ-2 has seen extensive combat service in Somalia, Bosnia, Kosovo, and Iraq. Currently, nine systems are serving in the active forces: five with the U.S. Navy, three operated by the Marine Corps, and one assigned to training.

In 1999, the hardware and software of the Pioneer UAV design were significantly upgraded. Although the RQ-2A was slated for replacement by newer UAV systems, program delays have allowed it to continue in U.S. Navy service to the present time.

This RQ-2 Pioneer has just touched down on the runway using the arresting hook to catch on the runway landing wire. The Pioneer saw heavy use during Operation Desert Storm in 1991. (U.S. Marine Corps)

Specifications (RQ-2B Model)

Length:	14 feet
Height:	3.9 feet
Wingspan:	16.9 feet
Weight:	452 pounds
Powerplant:	Sachs 2-stroke 2-cylinder piston engine 26hp
Maximum speed:	100 knots
Endurance:	5+ hours
Service ceiling:	15,000 feet

In 1958, Republic designed this reconnaissance UAV, the SD-3, for the U.S. Army, but after one prototype was built, the program was cancelled. The basic airframe layout was similar to the that of the later Pioneer UAV. (Republic archives via Cradle of Aviation)

The airframe layout and the rear engine location of the Pioneer UAV is strikingly similar to those of the 1958 Republic SD-3 UAV design shown in the photo to the left. (Ken Neubeck)

The RQ-2 Pioneer was used extensively in 1991 by both the U.S. Marines and U.S. Navy for various surveillance missions during Operation Desert Storm, accruing over 1,100 hours of flying time. This Pioneer is landing on a runway in Saudi Arabia in service for the Marine Corps 3rd RPV Platoon. (U.S. Marine photo by SSGT J.R. Ruark)

Several unique design features can be seen in this shot of the Pioneer RQ-2 UAV. A gimbaled camera assembly is mounted in the lower fuselage of the vehicle, which features a tricycle landing gear system. The Pioneer has a long wing span and a wide tail section. The extension hanging from the rear of the vehicle is the tail hook assembly that facilitates landing on carriers and short runways. The yellow extrusion over the top of the fuselage is the antenna that receives control command signals. The Pioneer even has landing lights located on the top of the vertical rudder sections and on the tip of the long wingspan. The engine is located at the rear of the fuselage. Even though the Pioneer was designated for retirement, it continues to serve with the U.S. Navy. (U.S. Navy photo by Photographer's Mate 2nd Class Daniel J. McLain)

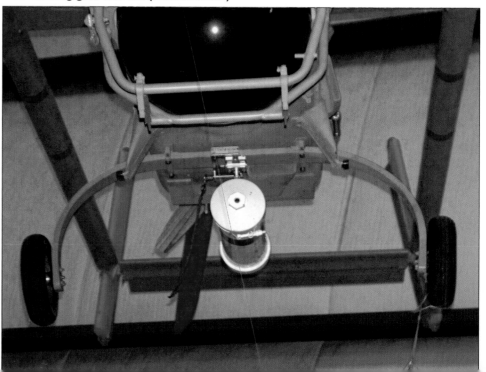

The orange trim painted on this Pioneer RQ-2 UAV, on display at the Patuxent Navy Air Museum in Maryland, marks it as a test vehicle. (Ken Neubeck)

A bracket assembly protects the front part of the glass dome that contains the camera. Located behind the dome are two UHF blade antennas. (Ken Neubeck)

This frontal view of the Pioneer displays the unique tricycle landing gear, the top antenna, the top of the rear propeller blade, and the dual vertical tail sections. (Ken Neubeck)

A JATO rocket booster is attached to the rear section of this Pioneer, just behind the main landing gear wheels. (Ken Neubeck)

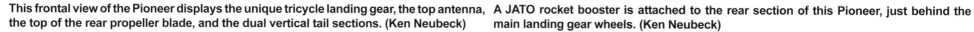

Sailors from the Firebees Fleet Composite Squadron are preparing to release an RQ-2 Pioneer during a 2005 demonstration at NAS in Patuxent River. (U.S. Navy Photo by Photographer's Mate 2nd Class Daniel J. McLain)

A Firebees Squadron Pioneer sails through the air at a demonstration at NAS in Patuxent River in 2005. The gimbaled camera in the lower fuselage is in operation. (US Navy Photo by Photographer's Mate 2nd Class Daniel J. McLain)

This Pioneer has just been launched from the battleship USS *Wisconsin* during Operation Desert Shield in 1991. It is in camouflage paint scheme to help it blend in with the terrain when it flies low. (U.S. Navy Photo by PH2 Carnes)

This Pioneer RQ-2 conducts surveillance over al-Anbâr Province during U.S. Marine operations in western Iraq in 2006. UAVs are highly suitable for certain surveillance tasks formerly handled by manned aircraft. (Sgt. Jennifer L. Jones / U.S. Marine Corps)

During takeoff from the ground, the Pioneer UAV is loaded at the base of a dual set of rails mounted at the back of an M-814 five-ton truck. (U.S. Marine Corps photo by Sgt. Jennifer L. Jones)

This Pioneer is in the middle of the launch sequence during takeoff from an M-814 five-ton truck in the California desert. The landing wheels of the UAV straddle the outside of the rails. (U.S. Marines photo by Lance Corporal E.J. Young)

This RQ-2A Pioneer, serving in Desert Storm in 1991, has been catapulted from the rails mounted on the truck and is off to perform its mission. (U.S. Marine Corps)

This Pioneer has cleared the launching truck in flight testing during Operation Desert Shield in 1991, prior to Operation Desert Storm. (U.S. Navy)

Eagle Eye VUAV

One of the more unusual UAVs to be tested by the U.S. Navy was the Eagle Eye, a tiltrotor UAV that was considered for the U.S. Navy VT-UAV program and that had a strong resemblance to the V-22 tiltrotor aircraft.

The Eagle Eye was manufactured by Bell and was intended as part of the suite of vehicles making up the U.S. Coast Guard's Intergrated Deepwater System Program that was originally proposed in 1993 for the policing of the territorial waters of the United States. In 1993, Bell kicked off this effort by manufacturing a 7/8th-scale prototype of the UAV that was originally designated the TR911X.

The two demonstrator aircraft was powered by a single Allison 250-C20 turboshaft engine that was mounted in the center of the fuselage, with a transmission system that drove rotor assemblies at the end of each wing. The UAV made its first flight in March of 1998, followed by a flight test program. Land-based operation testing, which was Phase 1, was completed in April of 1998, and Phase 2's sea-based testing started after that and was completed by the end of the century. The first prototype was destroyed in an accident in the course of the testing program, but the second prototype went on to finish the program, completing over 90 hours of flight time.

The success of the test program led to the construction of a full-scale model, designated TR918 in 2002. It was powered by a new, the Pratt & Whitney PW207D turboshaft engine. The U.S. Coast Guard considered the UAV for the service's Deepwater Program until funds were put on hold.

Since that time, Bell has continued to market the Eagle Eye to the U.S. Navy while submitting proposals for a variant to European countries. So far it has not obtained a significant production order, a failure that might in part be due to competition from another rotor-style design UAV, the Fire Scout, which is in full production. Indeed, the legacy of the Eagle Eye may be that it served as the bridge between the QH-50 rotorcraft and the Fire Scout in the history of this type of UAV for the U.S. Navy.

It was observed during the flight test program that the UAV required less than one hour of maintenance per flight hour, a good ratio that was due to designed-in features such as the folding nose, folding tail, and hinged engine cowl that afforded quick access.

The Eagle Eye UAV is a tilt rotor vehicle that was initially developed in 1993 and considered for the U.S. Coast Guard's Deepwater program. (U.S. Coast Guard)

One of the surviving demonstrators is displayed at the Patuxent River Naval Air Museum in Maryland. (Ken Neubeck)

Specifications

Length:	18.3 feet
Height:	6.1 feet
Wingspan:	24.1 feet
Empty weight:	3,836 pounds
Max takeoff weight:	2,250 pounds
Powerplant:	Pratt & Whitney PW207D Turboshaft
Maximum speed:	225 mph
Endurance:	6 hours
Service ceiling:	20,000 feet

The Eagle Eye has one set of landing gears in its nose section and one set in the middle of the fuselage. (Ken Neubeck)

A small wheel assembly is located at the bottom of the tilt rotor assemblies at the ends of the wings. (Ken Neubeck)

Located behind the top intake scoop is the engine exhaust vent. The antenna for receiving UHF signals is located below this vent on the lower fuselage (Ken Neubeck)

The tail consists of two vertical sections that curve up from the horizontal stabilizer section. (Ken Neubeck)

MQ-8 Fire Scout Rotary UAV

With the U.S. Navy planning to retire the RQ-2 Pioneers that were approaching the end of their service life, a search was initiated for a replacement UAV with additional capabilities such as vertical takeoff and landing, higher payload capability, and longer loiter time. Three companies participated in the competition for the contract to supply this new UAV, and in the year 2000, the Navy announced that the team of Teledyne Ryan and Schweizer Aircraft had won the deal.

The Fire Scout was a derivative of the Schweizer three-passenger, turbine powered 330SP helicopter with a modified fuselage, fuel system, UAV electronics, and sensors. The initial mission concept for the Fire Scout was for the UAV to find, identify, and track tactical targets both at sea and on land. The UAV was designed to land and take off from any aviation-capable warship as well as from unprepared landing areas.

Beneath the skin of this UAV, some Fire Scout elements strongly resembled components of the earlier U.S. Navy DASH. While both UAVs used rotors, the Fire Scout used a single set of blades, as compared with the dual rotors on the DASH. The Fire Scout used a tail rotor setup to provide additional stability, while the QH-50D DASH had dispensed with the tail altogether. Yet there were other features that were remarkably similar. The Fire Scout's landing strut design was very similar to that of the DASH, since both aircraft had to be able to land on U.S. Navy ships during rough seas. A jet-fueled Rolls Royce Allison 250-C20 turbine engine powered the Fire Scout. While patrolling within a 110-mile radius around its base ship, the Fire Scout was directed from control stations aboard the vessel.

The Fire Scout prototype flew for the first time in January of 2000; but then in November, the prototype crashed and was destroyed. In January of 2001, the program was put on hold and in December of 2001, funding for production of the Fire Scout was cut, even though progress had been satisfactory.

Despite this setback, over the next few years, Northrop Grumman (which had taken over Teledyne Ryan) continued to work on a variety of design improvements and developed a new version prototype to try to generate new interest. A major design change was the introduction of a four-blade rotor system in lieu of the original three-blade rotor in order to reduce noise as well as improve lift capacity. The new design also featured stub wings or sponsons that could help with carrying the Viper strike missile and various weapon pods that are capable of firing low-precision rockets.

The MQ-8B has an electro-optical camera with laser rangefinder and designator mounted in a turret assembly located in the lower fuselage toward the nose of the aircraft. This camera sends back real-time video images to the control station aboard ship.

Eventually in 2003, the U.S. Army became interested in the Fire Scout and awarded a contract for seven RQ-8B evaluation UAVs. In 2006, the Fire Scout was redesignated the MQ-8B. The M designation reflects the multi-functional roles that Fire Scout is now capable of playing, beyond the original R designation. The Army's interest in the project renewed interest by the U.S. Navy, which ordered nine Fire Scout MQ-8B derivatives for evaluation. Production of flight-test MQ-8B models for the Navy began in April of 2006

This early-model Fire Scout featuring a three-bladed main rotor undergoes testing in California. Future models would also feature left and right sponsons that would be used to hold armaments and other equipment. (Northrop Grumman)

and the first flight took place in December of 2006 at the Naval Air Station in Patuxent River.

Low-rate production of the MQ-8B began in May of 2007 with delivery slated for completion by the end of 2008. Although this UAV is expected to be deployed primarily on Navy Littoral Combat Ships, two Fire Scout MQ-8Bs have been assigned to the guided-missile frigate USS *McInerney* for drug interdiction missions off of South America. The deployment of these two UAVs will allow the Navy to complete operational evaluation and work out different operation concepts for the Fire Scout.

Specifications (MQ-8B Model)

Total length:	31.7 feet
Height:	9.8 feet
Empty weight:	2,073 pounds
Max takeoff weight:	3,150 pounds
Powerplant:	Rolls-Royce 250C20W turboshaft engine
Maximum speed:	125+ knots
Endurance:	5 hours with a 600 pound payload
Range:	110 miles
Service ceiling:	20,000 feet

This RQ-8A Fire Scout undergoes a series of developmental flight tests at the Webster Field Annex of the Naval Air Station (NAS) Patuxent River in late 2003. The Fire Scout completed 80 sorties and generally pleased the Navy. Nevertheless, funding cuts caused delays in the RQ-8A program. (U.S. Navy photo by Kurt Lengfield)

An RQ-8A Fire Scout prepares to land aboard the amphibious transport dock ship USS *Nashville* in January 2006. During this test, the Fire Scout provided coverage as far as 110 nautical miles from the launch site. This was the first autonomous landing of the Fire Scout aboard a Navy vessel at sea. (U.S. Navy photo by Kurt Lengfield)

Underneath the forward fuselage of the RQ-8A are an electro-optical camera and laser rangefinder. In front of the Modular Mission Payloads (MMP) is the UCARS antenna used in landing the UAV. (U.S. Navy photo by Photographer's Mate 2nd Class Daniel J. McLain)

The right missile launcher on an RQ-8A Fire Scout has just fired a 2.75-inch Mark 66 unguided rocket during weapons testing at the Yuma, Arizona, proving grounds. (Northrop Grumman)

This RQ-8A Fire Scout is configured in an attack mode setup with a pair of Mark-66 missile launchers mounted on brackets extending from both landing struts. The Fire Scout uses an Unmanned Aerial Vehicle Common Automatic Recovery System (UCARS) in order to land aboard ships. (U.S. Navy Photo by Photographer's Mate 2nd Class Daniel J. McLain)

When the Navy lost interest in the RQ-8A Fire Scout, Northrop Grumman continued with further design improvements to create the RQ-8B version that featured a four-bladed rotor for improved performance. (Northrop Grumman)

After testing, this RQ-8B prototype painted in Northrop Grumman colors and markings aroused the interest of the U.S. Army, which ordered evaluation units. The U.S. Navy soon followed suit and ordered its own evaluation units. (Northrop Grumman)

This U.S. Navy evaluation unit is painted gray. With the addition of stub wings for carrying ordnance, the Fire Scout was redesignated the MQ-8B, in recognition of the multiple missions that it could perform. (Northrop Grumman)

A probe for collecting performance data during flight testing has been attached to the left stub wing of this MQ-8B. The U.S. Navy tested this model at the Patuxent River NAS facility. (Northrop Grumman)

This airborne MQ-8B Fire Scout reveals a number of its details. There is a landing light near the rear of each sponson or stub wing. Two tie-down loops, one on each side of the craft, facilitate stowage aboard ship. On the bottom of the aircraft are strobe lights and vents through which engine exhaust is directed. The vertical rectangle in the middle of the fuselage is the engine's main intake filter. Fuel is stored in bladders located inside the extruded section that leads up to the rotor blades. In front of that structure is the forward TCDI omni antenna. There are UHF/VHF blade antennas on the bottom and top of the tail, and a strobe light and GPS antenna are also found atop the tail. (Northrop Grumman)

This MQ-8B Fire Scout is about to be loaded onto the frigate USS *McInerney* for active deployment in anti-drug trafficking operations in Latin America. (U.S. Navy photo by Mass Communication Specialist 1st Class Holly Boynton)

The assignment of this MQ-8B Fire Scout to the frigate USS *McInerney* serves the U.S. Navy risk reduction plan in anticipation of Littoral Combat Ship deployment. (U.S. Navy photo by Mass Communication Specialist 1st Class Holly Boynton)

This Fire Scout is one of two assigned to the USS *McInerney* for its first operational deployment. The test probe on the UAV's right sponson is designed to collect data. The U.S. Navy evaluated the two UAVs assigned to the ship as they assisted counter-drug operations conducted in South America in May of 2008. The similarity between the operation of the Fire Scout and the DASH QH-50 is striking. Like the DASH, the Fire Scout takes off and lands from the rear decks of Navy ships. The Navy has plans to deploy the Fire Scout for operations aboard the new littoral combat ships that are to become a major part of the fleet. (U.S. Navy photos by Mass Communication Specialist 2nd Class Alan Gragg)

RQ-4N Global Hawk UAV

The Global Hawk RQ-4 is the largest UAV in U.S. military service with the RQ-4N being the designation for the U.S. Navy version. The aircraft has a massive wingspan of over 116 feet and can stay aloft for up to 36 hours, making it ideal for long maritime surveillance patrols.

Like some of the other UAVs, the Global Hawk traces its lineage to an earlier manned aircraft design: the U-2 spy plane of the 1950s. The Global Hawk RQ-4 was originally developed for the United States Air Force (USAF) for which it has successfully performed a number of missions in Iraq. Eventually, the U.S. Navy became interested in this UAV platform for the performance of long-duration maritime surveillance.

In 2006, two Global Hawk RQ-4A UAVs from the Block 10 production lot for the USAF were transferred to the U.S. Navy for evaluation. Designated N-1, the two aircraft were tested in naval configuration, with one aircraft being evaluated at Edwards AFB from 2006 to 2008, when it was transferred to NAS at Patuxent River. The aircraft took part in Naval exercises in the Pacific and helped battle the Northern California wildfires in 2008.

Based on this evaluation, the Navy put out a contract proposal called Broad Area Maritime Surveillance (BAMS) for a UAV to conduct maritime intelligence, surveillance, and reconnaissance (ISR). This type of mission had formerly been handled by the P-3 Orion but the Navy was considering use of the new P-8 Poseidon aircraft with a UAV platform to take over the job. Three teams, Northrop Grumman, Lockheed Martin, and Boeing, submitted proposals for BAMS and in April of 2008, the U.S. Navy awarded Northrop Grumman the BAMS system development program contract.

Just a few weeks later, however, in May, Lockheed Martin protested the contract award, saying that its Mariner UAV, which was based on Lockheed Martin's Predator B UAV, was cheaper and more effective. This dispute held up the award of the contract until August of 2008, when the GAO upheld the award to Northrop Grumman, citing the firm's better technical proposal and better past performance with UAVs. The Navy felt that three RQ-4N jet-powered UAVs would provide better service than four turboprop Mariners UAVs. Under the contract, a total of 68 aircraft are to be delivered by 2015 at a cost of $55 million each. With this contract award, it is expected that the Australian Navy will also be buying RQ-4N aircraft for its maritime surveillance program.

The RQ-4N incorporates a maritime radar that has full 360° coverage around the vehicle and has an electronically scanned array and electro-optical infrared ball turret in its nose. The RQ-4N will have electronic support measure capability that will allow it to detect incoming electronic signals from other weapon systems. In addition, the RQ-4N will use a communications suite that, like that of the USAF RQ-4, will be able to use military satellite communications.

The RQ-4N will typically fly at very high altitudes, above all commercial and most military aircraft, thus reducing the risk of collision or airspace conflict. In addition, the wind levels at the higher altitudes are lower, which will benefit the turbofan propulsion system with better fuel economy and allow for longer mission duration.

An RQ-4A Global Hawk demonstrator (N-1 model) for the U.S. Navy undergoes testing at Edwards AFB in California, prior to its transfer to NAS in Patuxent River in 2008 for more testing. (Northrop Grumman)

During the summer of 2009, one of the two N-1 model UAVs that was owned by the U.S. Navy at that time was sent to the Persian Gulf region to conduct operational field testing. The N-1 model flew more than 60 flights, accumulating 1,000 flight hours while providing images to the U.S. military forces deployed in that complex region.

The N-1 model was controlled by U.S. Navy personnel who were operating back in Patuxent River, Maryland. This UAV returned to the United States in October of 2009 for depot-level maintenance. Meanwhile, the other RQ-4N was sent for duty overseas.

Specifications (N-1 model)

Length:	44.4 feet
Height:	15.1 feet
Wingspan:	116.1 feet
Empty weight:	8,490 pounds
Max takeoff weight:	22,900 pounds
Powerplant:	Rolls-Royce AE3007H turbofan engine
Cruise speed:	404 mph
Endurance:	36 hours
Range:	12,000 nautical miles
Service ceiling:	65,000 feet

This is Global Hawk tail number 166510, one of two N-1 evaluator aircraft transferred from USAF to the Navy. Its long wings allow it to loiter for a long period over a target area. (Paul Negri)

The N-1 first took to the air as a maritime demonstration unit in October of 2004, flying for four hours from Northrop Grumman's Palmdale facility to Edwards AFB. (Northrop Grumman)

One of the N-1 evaluators is seen during a flight test by the U.S. Navy at Edwards AFB. Flight testing at Edwards was conducted from 2004 through 2006. (Northrop Grumman)

An N-1 evaluator aircraft takes off from Edwards AFB in March of 2006 for a cross-country flight to NAS in Patuxent River for further evaluation by the Navy for the BAMS mission. (USAF photo by Chad Bellay)

This N-1 Global Hawk evaluation aircraft, one of the two Global Hawks transferred to the Navy, undergoes flight testing over the desert near Edwards AFB in 2006. The paint scheme for this aircraft is dark gray for the fuselage with white colored wings. Production aircraft for the BAMS program will be painted in an all-gray paint scheme. (Northrop Grumman)

Parked at Edwards AFB, the Navy's evaluation Global Hawk RQ-4A (foreground) and the USAF RQ-4B Global Hawk (behind it) look identical. The electronics inside them, however, reflect their different roles. The evaluation RQ-4A UAV uses Navy-unique sensor and communications suites for data collection. A ball turret housing an electro-optical infrared assembly is to replace the turret in its nose. (Northrop Grumman)

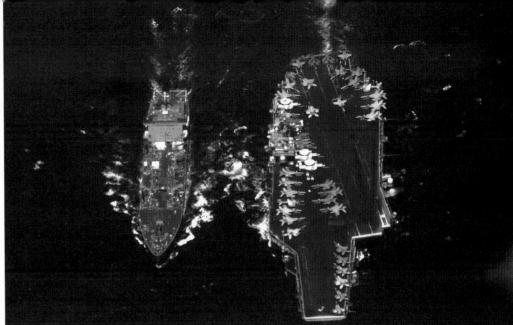

This image of the USS *Kitty Hawk* and a supply ship was shot in July 2008 by a Global Hawk during its flight to the Pacific Rim, where it participated in various exercises during an eight-week deployment from Pt. Magu in California. (U.S. Navy)

A Global Hawk's camera shot this image of the wildfires in Northern California during its support of firefighting efforts in July 2008. (U.S. Navy)

This artist's rendition of a production version RQ-4N Global Hawk shows the well-known hawk symbol painted on the tail of the aircraft, signifying its surveillance role. Its ball turret is different from the N-1 evaluation units' turret design. The initial contract for the BAMS program for the U.S. Navy is for three aircraft. Production is estimated to reach a total of 68 aircraft by the year 2015 at a cost of $55 million each. (Northrop Grumman)

X-47B Pegasus UCAV

The X-47B Pegasus is a demonstration unmanned combat aerial vehicle (UCAV) that Northrop Grumman is developing for the U.S. Navy as a carrier-based attack UAV.

The original vehicle was designated X-47A and was developed on the basis of Northrup Grumman's private funding. This aircraft competed against the Boeing X-45A for the Defense Advance Research Project Agency (DARPA) Joint Unmanned Combat Air System program (J-UCAS). The first flight of the X-45A was in May of 2002 and the X-47A's first flight was in February of 2003.

When the U.S. Air Force cancelled the J-UCAS program in 2006, the U.S. Navy continued evaluation of the two competing designs for the Unmanned Combat Air System carrier demonstration (UCAS-D) program. In August of 2007, the Navy awarded the USCAS-D program to the Northrop Grumman X-47B Pegasus. The X-47B is a significantly larger and heavier aircraft than the X-47A version, with the length going from 27.9 feet to 38.2 feet, the wingspan growing from 27.8 feet to 62.1 feet, and the weight increasing significantly to 42,000 pounds. These changes to size and weight are meant to make the Pegasus capable of serving as an unmanned bomber aircraft that would be launched and recovered from an aircraft carrier.

The Pegasus demonstrator resembles the B-2 Spirit bomber and uses a retractable tricycle landing gear. The X-47A is powered by a Pratt & Whitney Canada JT15D-5C turbofan engine. The B-model, however, will be powered by a Pratt & Whitney F100-220 engine. The X-47A has two weapons bays, one on each side of the engine. These bays are loaded with a single 500-pound dummy bomb to simulate flight loads during test flights. In addition, flight landing on carrier deck was evaluated and a nose-landing gear attachment was added to facilitate carrier launch.

The USCAS-D program includes the construction of two X-47B vehicles that will be evaluated during a three-year test program to be conducted at both Edwards AFB and NAS Patuxent River. Sea trials are to be held in November 2011. Rollout of the first demonstrator X-47B took place in December of 2009. Although the Boeing X-45 Phantom Ray lost the original USCAS-D competition, Boeing has used private company funding to revive the project and continue to seek new business.

Specifications (X-47A Model)

Length:	27.4 feet
Height:	6.1 feet
Wingspan:	27.8 feet
Empty weight:	3,836 pounds
Max takeoff weight:	5,905 pounds
Powerplant:	Pratt & Whitney JT15D05C
Cruise speed:	high subsonic
Range:	1,500 nautical miles
Service ceiling:	40,000 feet

Northrop Grumman built the X-47A mockup prior to making the prototype model that flew against the Boeing X-45A prototype. (Ken Neubeck)

This X-45C Phantom Ray demonstrator built by Boeing competed unsuccessfully against the X-47B Pegasus for the U.S. Navy UCAS-D program in 2007. The weapons bay doors are open and dummy bombs are extended. (Paul Negri)

This X-47A Pegasus mockup is located in the Patuxent River Naval Air Museum in Maryland. (Ken Neubeck)

The surfaces of the Pegasus are smooth throughout the aircraft, including the area where the wings meet the fuselage section. (Ken Neubeck)

There is a single door that is hinged in front of the nose landing gear. (Ken Neubeck)

The Pegasus can be towed using the tow bar attachment. (Ken Neubeck)

Two door sections flank each of the two main landing gears. (Ken Neubeck)

There is a scissors assembly on each landing gear strut. (Ken Neubeck)

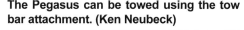

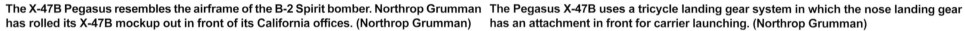

The X-47B Pegasus resembles the airframe of the B-2 Spirit bomber. Northrop Grumman has rolled its X-47B mockup out in front of its California offices. (Northrop Grumman)

The Pegasus X-47B uses a tricycle landing gear system in which the nose landing gear has an attachment in front for carrier launching. (Northrop Grumman)

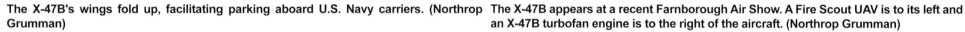

The X-47B's wings fold up, facilitating parking aboard U.S. Navy carriers. (Northrop Grumman)

The X-47B appears at a recent Farnborough Air Show. A Fire Scout UAV is to its left and an X-47B turbofan engine is to the right of the aircraft. (Northrop Grumman)

ScanEagle UAV

The ScanEagle UAV is a portable UAV that has many applications for the U.S. Navy. ScanEagle has been developed jointly by Boeing and Insitu UAV, based on a previously produced civilian UAV known as SeaScan, which was used for collecting weather data and for tracking tuna for commercial fishing purposes. ScanEagle is a small vehicle that can be launched from just about anywhere at sea or on the land.

Weighing only 38 pounds, ScanEagle is just four feet long, has a 10-foot wingspan, and can be carried and launched easily. As standard payload for conducting surveillance and reconnaissance assignments, ScanEagle packs either an inertially stabilized electro-optical camera for daylight work or an infrared camera for use at night. It can operate within a communication range of over 100km, and has a flight endurance of 20 hours. Scan Eagle's maximum speed is 75 knots (139km/h).

ScanEagle can be launched without an airfield using a pneumatic launcher and can be recovered by using the "SkyHook" retrieval system. At the end of the wingtip of the aircraft is a hook, which catches a rope attached to a 30- to 50-foot pole on the top of which is a GPS mechanism.

Among the military services using ScanEagle in April 2005 was the U.S. Navy, which in that month awarded Boeing a $14.5 million contract to provide UAV services in support of Operation Iraqi Freedom and the Global War on Terror. Under the deal Boeing supplies ScanEagle UAVs, communication links, and ground equipment to support Navy requirements. ScanEagle is assigned to a number of Navy destroyers and has been a key surveillance tool in anti-piracy sea patrols, particularly in the waters off East Africa.

In addition, Boeing is providing ScanEagle UAVs with communication links and ground equipment for Naval Expeditionary Strike Group (ESG) and oil platform security in the Persian Gulf. Additional contracts were awarded to Boeing in September 2005 to provide ScanEagle system support for Navy high-speed vessels as well as a floating forward staging base. ScanEagle is also used by the Australian Army.

ScanEagle has flown over 150,000 combat hours and facilitated over 1,500 captures at sea, while achieving a 99-percent mission readiness rate for both land and sea.

Because of its small size, the ScanEagle UAV has proven very useful in situations outside of traditional battlefields. In one such instance, the UAV provided surveillance of the hostage situation in the seas off of Somalia in April of 2009.

Specifications

Length:	4 feet
Wingspan:	10 feet
Gross weight:	40 pounds
Powerplant:	1 x 1.9 KW 3W-28 piston engine
Cruise speed:	48 mph
Endurance:	15+ hours
Service ceiling:	16,000 feet

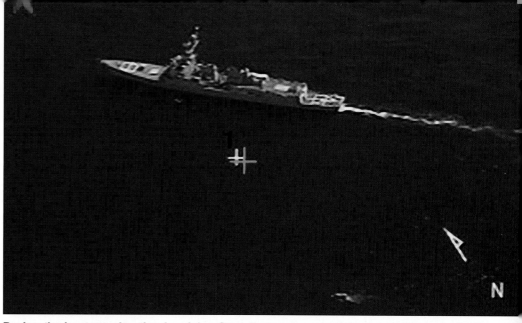

During the hostage situation involving Somali pirates and a U.S. cargo ship in April of 2009, a ScanEagle UAV was launched from the U.S. Navy Destroyer *Bainbridge* (shown at the top of the photo) in order to provide photo surveillance of the lifeboat (seen at the bottom of the photo) where pirates were holding the captain of the freighter *Maersk Alabama* hostage. (U.S. Navy)

An Insitu Company operator on the ship is using a computer to control a ScanEagle during a U.S. Department of State support mission to assess earthquake damage in the Solomon Islands. (U.S. Navy photo by Mass Communication Specialist 2nd Class Andrew Meyers)

A ScanEagle UAV launches from the Navy Surface Warfare Center Dahlgren test range. (US Navy photo by John F. Williams)

A Boeing field representative is preparing a ScanEagle for a mission to be launched from Navy ship *Stockham* to assess tsunami damage on the Solomon Islands. (U.S. Navy photo by Mass Communications Specialist 2nd Class Andrew Meyers)

This close-up view of the front of the ScanEagle UAV shows the camera inside a glass assembly. The camera is on a gimbaled assembly that allows the operator to track both stationary and moving targets. (U.S. Navy photo by Photographer's Mate 2nd Class Daniel J. McLain)

Boeing company personnel prepare to load a ScanEagle on a pneumatic wedge catapult launcher during training at the Marine Corps Air Station in Yuma, Arizona. (U.S. Marine Corps photo by Cpl. Michael P. Snody)

A ScanEagle UAV is successfully launched from the catapult launcher, which can also be used on U.S. Navy ships. (U.S. Marine Corps photo by Michael P. Snody)

During training at Yuma, Arizona, a Boeing mechanic operator retrieves a ScanEagle using a skyhook, a rope on a pole that catches the UAV out of mid-air. The skyhook can also be used on U.S. Navy ships. (Guadalupe M. Deanda III. / U.S. Marine Corps)

A ScanEagle is recovered from flight onboard the destroyer USS *Oscar Austin* while at sea. (U.S. Navy photo by Mass Communication Special 3rd Class Michelle L. Kapica)

A ScanEagle is launched from the flight deck of the USS *Saipan* using a catapult launcher. The ScanEagle is capable of remaining in flight for 20 hours or more at a time at a cruising speed of 75 knots. (U.S. Navy photo by Mass Communications Specialist Seaman Patrick W. Mullen III)

ScanEagle is recovered after its flight on the deck of the USS *Saipan* amphibious assault ship while on routine deployment. Typically, a crew of two personnel is needed to capture the ScanEagle using the recovery device on deck. (U.S. Navy photo by Mass Communication Specialist Seaman Patrick W. Mullen III)

RQ-16 T-HAWK

The Honeywell T-Hawk is at the forefront of a new class of UAV known as Micro Air Vehicles (MAVs). The T-Hawk is a ducted fan VTOL MAV that is suitable for backpack deployment and single-person operation. It is a major platform that is currently seeing much service in Iraq and Afghanistan in the search for roadside bombs.

The MAV program was originally launched by the Defense Advance Research Project Agency (DARPA) with a $40 million technology demonstration contract awarded to Honeywell in 2003. Eventually the U.S. Army expressed interest in the MAV idea and the UAV that became the RQ-16, slowly started to evolve.

In 2007, the U.S. Navy gave Honeywell a $7.5 million contract for 20 Shadow UAVs for the purpose of deploying them into Iraq in support of the Marine Corps' critical mission of scanning the roads for roadside bombs. For a typical mission, the MAV would generally fly ahead of military convoys and scan the roads for any evidence of disturbed ground or suspicious structures. The UAV hovers at close range and it can cover more ground at a faster rate than an unmanned ground vehicle performing the same mission. The relatively small size and low weight of the MAV allows for easy transport by military personnel.

Because of the success of the MAV in Iraq, the U.S. Navy placed an unexpected order for 372 more RQ-16As in January 2008. Each system consists of two MAVs and one ground station, meaning that there would be a total of 186 MAV systems.

The T-Hawk MAV is one of a new class of UAVs that is proving its worth on the battlefields of Iraq and Afghanistan. (U.S. Navy)

The RQ-16 T-Hawk is used by both the U.S. Army and Navy. (U.S. Army)

Specifications

Length:	2 feet
Height:	2 feet (approximate)
Wingspan:	1.1 feet
Empty Weight:	5 pounds
Max takeoff Weight:	17 pounds
Powerplant:	Boxer twin piston engine 4HP
Maximum speed:	57 mph
Endurance:	50+ minutes
Service ceiling:	10,500 feet

THE FUTURE

UAV is the wave of the future for many military applications, replacing those missions that were previously conducted by manned aircraft. UAVs are especially effective for those manned aircraft missions that were either tedious or dangerous. In addition, a number of missions will involve the incorporation of both manned aircraft and UAVs working together. All four branches of the U.S. Military, the Air Force, the Army, the Navy and the Marines, are involved in the use of UAVs.

The world of the UAV is growing and changing rapidly, making it very hard to capture all of the latest models that are coming out. At the time of this writing, there are several dozen manufacturers worldwide that make UAVs in over 100 different models. In addition, there are many subcontractors making different mechanical and electrical components for the UAVs.

Future design will require some additional engineering to prevent enemy capture of video information and interference with UAV control signals. There was a situation in Iraq in 2009 where insurgents were able to capture video information from UAVs using commercial off-the-shelf software. This pointed out the need for additional design refinements and the possible need for encryption of video and control signals for interference-free and protected operation of the UAV.

A member of the U.S. Army's 101st Military Intelligence Battalion prepares a Shadow 200 Unmanned Aerial Vehicle for launch at Forward Operating Base Warhorse near Ba'qûbah, Diyâlá Province, Iraq, during Operation Iraqi Freedom in September of 2004. (U.S. Army photo by Spc. James B. Smith Jr.)

KillerBee UAV is an intelligence gathering system and is seen here being launched in the desert. The UAV has a wingspan of 10 feet and weighs 30 pounds. It is being developed for all U.S. armed services, including the Navy. (Northrop Grumman)

The Silver Fox is a low-cost UAV that can provide video imaging during aerial surveillance. (Photographer's Mate 2nd Class Daniel J. McLain / U.S. Navy)

Engineers work on the U.S. Navy-built Guardian Griffin during flight testing in Virginia in 2006. The UAV is designed for several Navy missions. (John Joyce / U.S. Navy)

A Manta UAV takes off from the flight deck of the experimental boat *Stiletto* during testing near San Diego for usefulness in littoral combat and interoperable environments in 2006. (Photographer's Mate Airman Damien Horvath / U.S. Navy)

The Neptune RQ-15A UAV has a seven-foot wingspan and can be launched from small vessels and recovered in open water. A production order of 75 systems for special operations use began in 2002. (Daniel J. McLain / U.S. Navy)

The JB-2 Loon was developed from reverse engineering of the German V-1 rockets during World War II. The Loon was successfully launched from U.S. Navy ships and submarines in 1947.

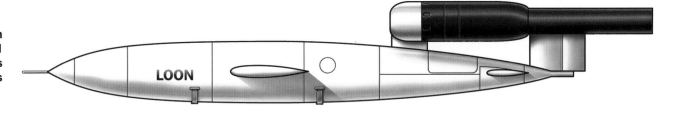

The Regulus Cruise missile was one of the first guided missiles to be used by the U.S. Navy and had features that are found on present-day UAVs. It is painted in U.S. Navy dark blue colors with the white lettering that was prevalent during the early 1950s.

The Firebee BQM-34 was and still is the most widely used target drone in US military service. Typical colors for U.S. Navy models are orange with a black nose as shown here or all gray with a black nose. The Navy marking and serial numbers are also painted on the drone.

The Chukar BQM-74 is another widely used target drone in U.S. Navy service. All models are painted in bright orange with a white nose as shown here. The bright orange paint scheme allows for easier spotting in the water, thus aiding quick recovery after mission completion.

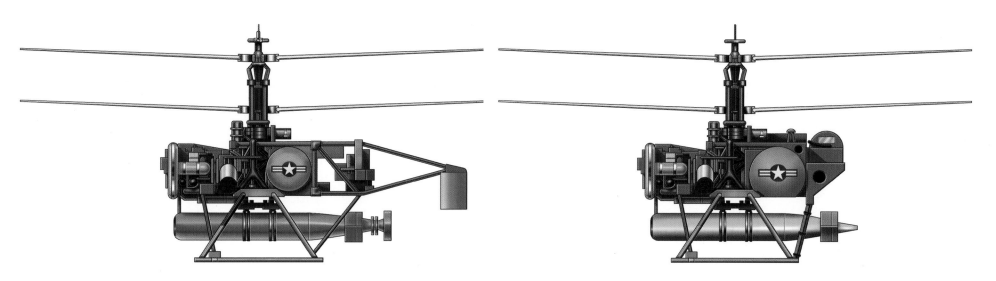

The QH-50 DASH UAV had two major configurations during production: the QH-50C model (left) with an extended tail section and the QH-50D model (right) without tail section. Both models had the same paint scheme for the rails and airframe, bright red on the left side of the UAV and bright green for the right side of the UAV.

The Pioneer RQ-2 is painted in light gray colors with U.S. insignia and black Navy marking on the fuselage. The UAV served extensively during Operation Desert Storm in 1991 achieving significant success as a target spotter for U.S. Navy ship guns. The Pioneer remains in U.S. Navy service up to the present time.

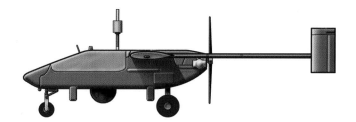

The U.S. Navy tested the ScanEagle for the U.S. Marine Corps. It is painted in light gray and has the Marines marking in black.

A number of units of the RQ-8A Fire Scout were evaluated by the U.S. Navy but no further production resulted. The UAV uses a three-bladed rotor, has no wing stubs, and is painted in light gray with black U.S. Navy markings.

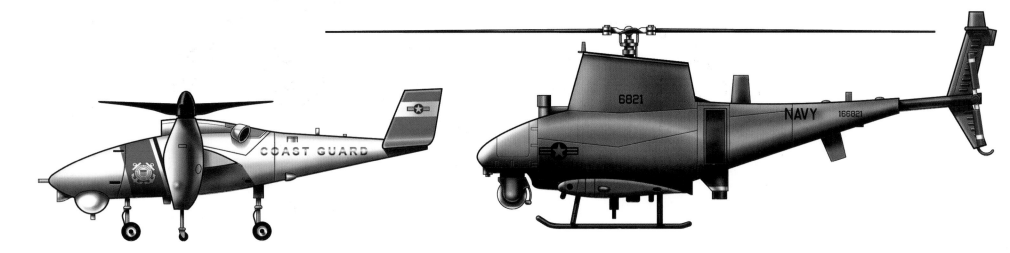

The Eagle Eye was a tiltrotor UAV that Bell developed during the 1990s for the U.S. Coast Guard's Deepwater Program. Funding for the program was put on hold but the company is still actively marketing this UAV.

The MQ-8B Fire Scout model aroused U.S. Navy interest and will go into production for service on U.S. Navy Littoral ships. This UAV uses a four-bladed rotor and has wing stubs for attaching ordnance. Additional blade antennas are added to the lower tail section from the previous model. The UAV is painted in medium gray with black U.S. Navy markings.

Two X-47 Pegasus UAVs are currently under evaluation by the U.S. Navy for carrier deployment and other missions. Sea trials begin in 2011.

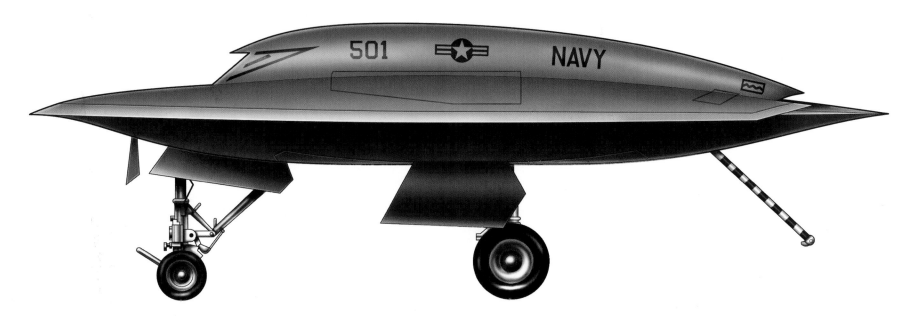

This is one of two N-1 Global Hawk UAVs that were evaluated by the U.S. Navy for feasibility in the Maritime Intelligence, Surveillance, and Reconnaissance (ISR) mission. The fuselage is painted blue-gray, the wings are white, and it displays U.S. Navy markings.

The RQ-4N production Global Hawk will be painted in all medium gray with U.S. Navy Markings and the hawk symbol on the rear tail section. Production is to continue through 2015 and the Navy is to take delivery of 68 UAVs.

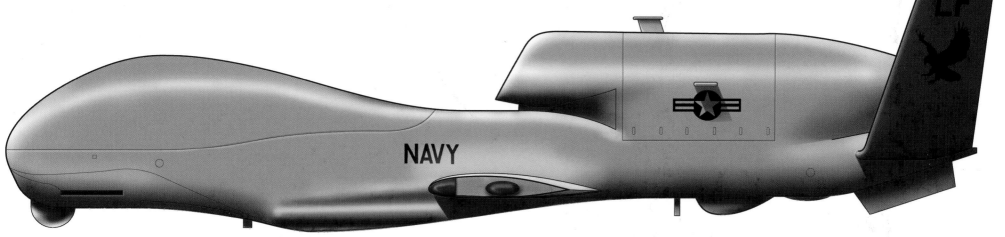

Sailors remove a Pioneer RQ-2 from the recovery net at the stern of the battleship USS *Iowa* during field testing in November 1986. The Pioneer RQ-2 can be launched either from a ship or from the land by use of a rocket launcher. U.S. Navy vessels used the Pioneer to spot potential threats in the form of enemy surface vehicles in addition to spotting potential targets on land for the guns of battleships. During Operation Desert Storm, the Pioneer was so effective in the latter role that Iraqi forces would surrender at the sound and sight of the UAV, knowing it was a prelude to Naval gun salvoes. (PHC Jeff Hilton / U.S. Navy)